Faber Studio Co.
Selections from BigTime® Piano

Arranged by Nancy and Randall Faber

This book belongs to: _____

Popular

Classics

Jazz & Blues

Rock 'n Roll

and more...

Production Coordinator: Jon Ophoff
Design and Illustration: Terpstra Design, San Francisco
Engraving: Dovetree Productions, Inc.

FABER
PIANO ADVENTURES®
3042 Creek Drive
Ann Arbor, Michigan 48108

A NOTE TO TEACHERS

The **Faber Studio Collections** offer a mix of styles with selections from the *PreTime®* to *BigTime®* Piano Supplementary Library. This sampling from the *Popular, Classics, Jazz & Blues, Rock 'n Roll*, and other favorite books presents an array of genres at each level. When a style resonates, the student can pick up just the right book for follow-up.

The **BigTime® Faber Studio Collection** is part of the *BigTime® Piano* series. "BigTime" designates Level 4 of the *PreTime®* to *BigTime® Piano Supplementary Library* arranged by Faber and Faber.

Following are the levels of the supplementary library, which lead from *PreTime®* to *BigTime®*.

PreTime® Piano	(Primer Level)
PlayTime® Piano	(Level 1)
ShowTime® Piano	(Level 2A)
ChordTime® Piano	(Level 2B)
FunTime® Piano	(Level 3A – 3B)
BigTime® Piano	(Level 4 and above)

Each level offers books in a variety of styles, making it possible for the teacher to offer stimulating material for every student. For a complimentary detailed listing, e-mail faber@pianoadventures.com or write us at the mailing address below.

Visit **www.PianoAdventures.com**.

ONLINE SUPPORT

Visit **www.PianoAdventures.com/studio** to find online support for this book!

ISBN 978-1-61677-645-9

Copyright © 2013 by Dovetree Productions, Inc.
c/o FABER PIANO ADVENTURES, 3042 Creek Dr., Ann Arbor, MI 48108
International Copyright Secured.   All Rights Reserved.   Printed in U.S.A.
WARNING: The music, text, design, and graphics in this publication are protected by copyright law.
Any duplication is an infringement of U.S. copyright law.

FF30

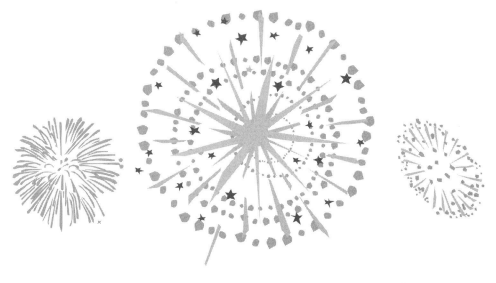

TABLE OF CONTENTS

Canon in D

JOHANN PACHELBEL
(1653-1706)

This arrangement © 1991 Dovetree Productions, Inc., c/o FABER PIANO ADVENTURES
International Copyright Secured.   All Rights Reserved.

FF302

The Pink Panther

from *THE PINK PANTHER*

Music by
HENRY MANCINI

swing the 8ths

Copyright © 1964 NORTHRIDGE MUSIC CO. and EMI U CATALOG INC. Copyright Renewed.
This arrangement Copyright © 2012 NORTHRIDGE MUSIC CO. and EMI U CATALOG INC.
All Rights for NORTHRIDGE MUSIC CO. Controlled and Administered by UNIVERSAL MUSIC CORP.
Exclusive Print Rights for EMI U CATALOG INC. Controlled and Administered by ALFRED MUSIC.
All Rights Reserved.   Used by Permission.

FF302

F3021

Can You Feel the Love Tonight

from Walt Disney's *The Lion King*

Music by ELTON JOHN
Lyrics by TIM RICE

Copyright © 1994 Wonderland Music Company, Inc.
This arrangement Copyright © 2003, 2012 Wonderland Music Company, Inc.
All Rights Reserved.   Used by Permission.

FF302

Additional Lyrics

There's a time for everyone, if they only learn
That the twisting kaleidoscope moves us all in turn.
There's a rhyme and reason to the wild outdoors
When the heart of this star-crossed voyager beats in time with yours. *To Chorus*

14

FF30

Morning Has Broken

TRADITIONAL

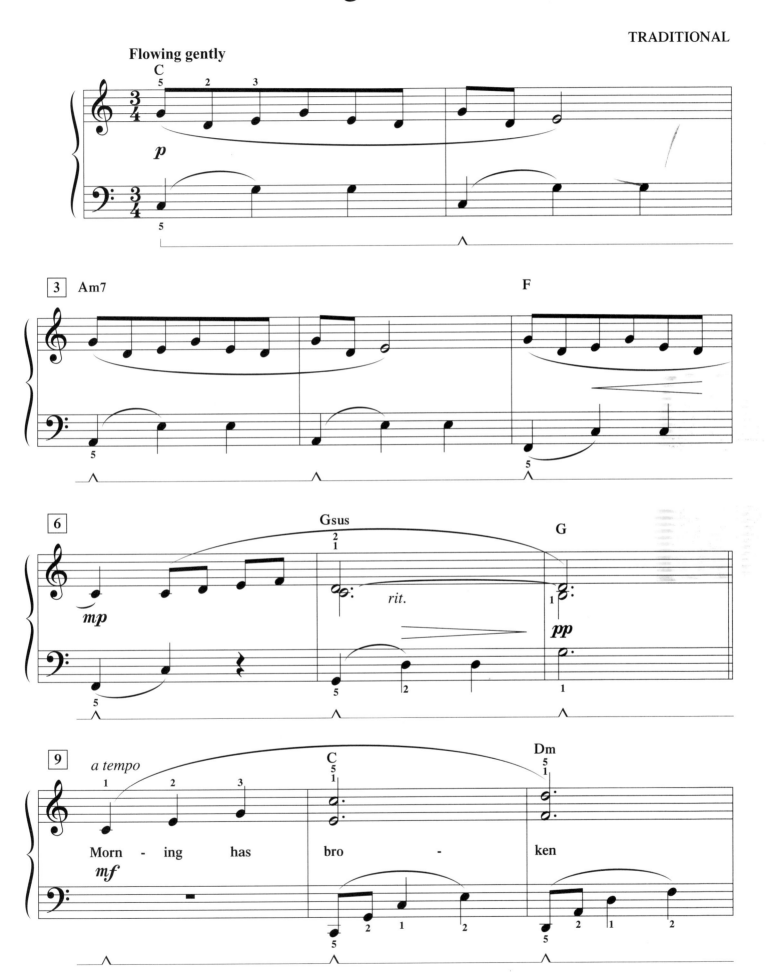

This arrangement © 1998 Dovetree Productions, Inc., c/o FABER PIANO ADVENTURES
International Copyright Secured.   All Rights Reserved.

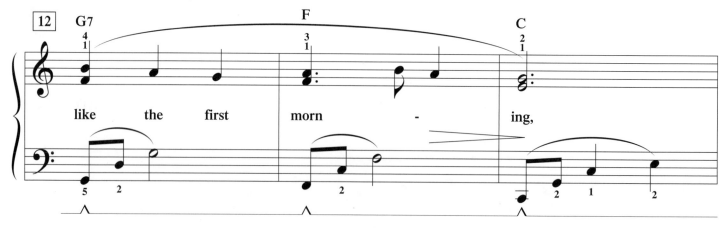

like the first morn - ing,

Black - bird has spo - ken

like the first bird.

Praise for his sing - ing,

FF302

Morning Has Broken

Favorites

TRADITIONAL

Morn - ing has bro - ken

Rock Around the Clock

Words by
MAX C. FREEDMAN

Music by
JIMMY DeKNIGHT

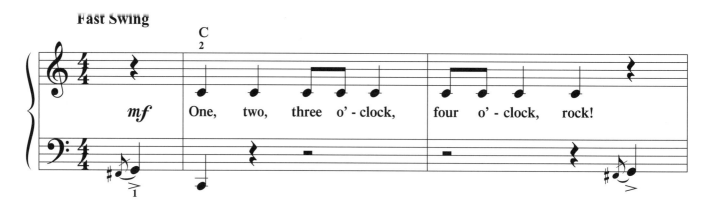

One, two, three o'-clock, four o'-clock, rock!

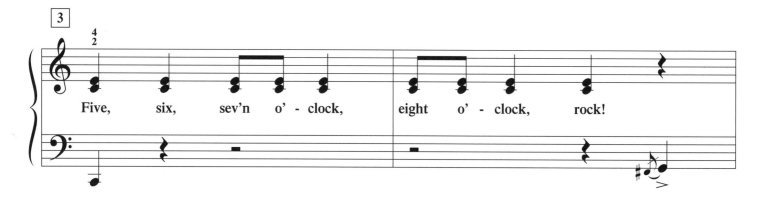

Five, six, sev'n o'-clock, eight o'-clock, rock!

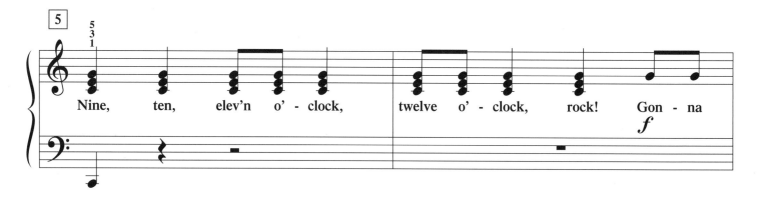

Nine, ten, elev'n o'-clock, twelve o'-clock, rock! Gon-na

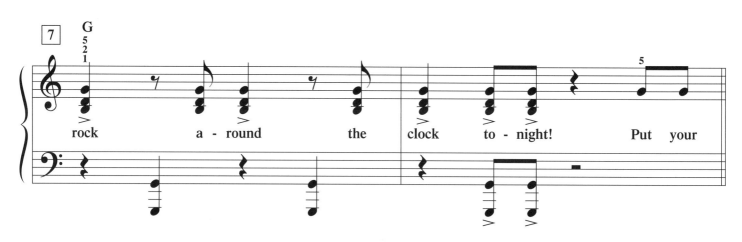

rock a - round the clock to - night! Put your

Copyright © 1953 Myers Music Inc., Kassner Associated Publishers Ltd. and Capano Music. Copyright Renewed.
This arrangement Copyright © 1990 and 1999 Myers Music Inc., Kassner Associated Publishers Ltd. and Capano Music.
All Rights on behalf of Myers Music Inc. and Kassner Associated Publishers Ltd. Administered by
Sony/ATV Music Publishing LLC, 8 Music Square West, Nashville, TN 37203.
International Copyright Secured.   All Rights Reserved.   Used by Permission.

FF302

100 Years

Words and Music by
JOHN ONDRASIK

Copyright © 2004 EMI BLACKWOOD MUSIC INC. and FIVE FOR FIGHTING MUSIC.
This arrangement Copyright © 2010 EMI BLACKWOOD MUSIC INC. and FIVE FOR FIGHTING MUSIC.
All Rights Controlled and Administered by EMI BLACKWOOD MUSIC INC.
International Copyright Secured.   All Rights Reserved.   Used by Permission.

FF3021

FF3021

Autumn Leaves

English lyrics by JOHNNY MERCER
French lyrics by JACQUES PREVERT

Music by
JOSEPH KOSMA

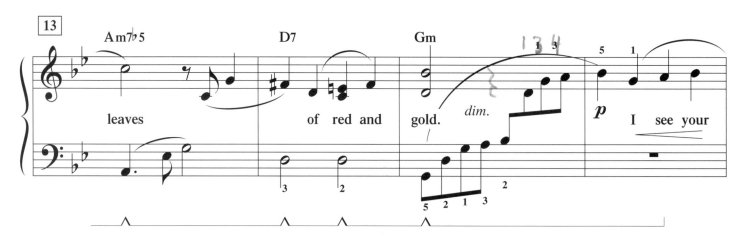

Copyright © 1947, 1950 (Renewed) ENOCH ET CIE.
This arrangement Copyright © 2011 ENOCH ET CIE.
Sole Selling Agent for U.S. and Canada: MORLEY MUSIC CO., by agreement with ENOCH ET CIE.
All Rights Reserved.   Used by Permission.

FF3021

lips,   the sum - mer   kiss - es,   the sun - burned

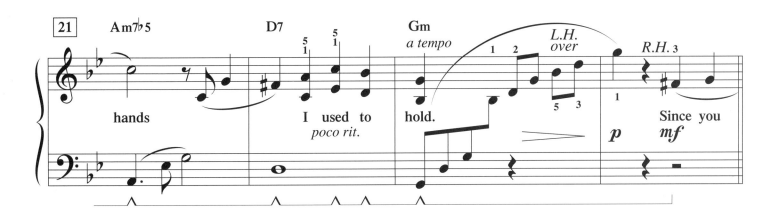

hands   I used to   hold.   Since you

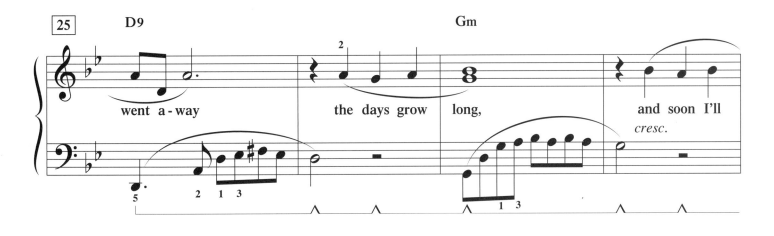

went a - way   the days grow   long,   and soon I'll

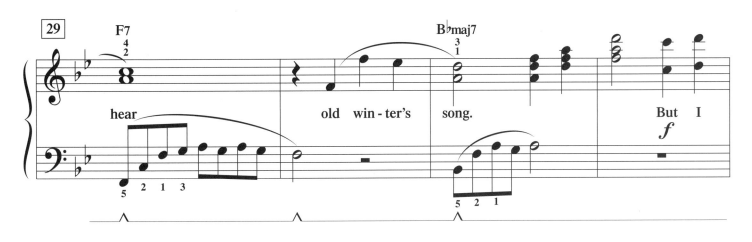

hear   old win - ter's   song.   But I

28

Deep River

Slowly, soulfully

Spiritual

Deep _____ riv - er, my

home is o - ver Jor - dan.

Deep _____ riv - er, Lord, I

want to cross o - ver in - to camp - ground.

This arrangement © 2004 Dovetree Productions, Inc., c/o FABER PIANO ADVENTURES
International Copyright Secured. All Rights Reserved.

Solace

Very slow march time (♩ = 80-84)

SCOTT JOPLIN

This arrangement © 1996 Dovetree Productions, Inc., c/o FABER PIANO ADVENTURES
International Copyright Secured.   All Rights Reserved.

FF302

Gangnam Style

Words and Music by
GUN HYUNG YOO and JAI SANG PARK

Dance Rock

Copyright © 2012 UNIVERSAL TUNES and SONY/ATV MUSIC PUBLISHING H.K. KOREA
This arrangement Copyright © 2013 UNIVERSAL TUNES and SONY/ATV MUSIC PUBLISHING H.K. KOREA
All Rights for UNIVERSAL TUNES Controlled and Administered by SONGS OF UNIVERSAL, INC.
All Rights for SONY/ATV MUSIC PUBLISHING H.K. KOREA in the U.S. and Canada Controlled and Administered by
SONY/ATV MUSIC PUBLISHING LLC, 8 Music Square West, Nashville, TN 37203.
All Rights Reserved.   Used by Permission.

FF302